The Green Piano

Books by Janine Pommy Vega

POETRY

Poems to Fernando (1968)
Journal of a Hermit (1974)
Morning Passage (1976)
Here at the Door (1978)
Journal of a Hermit & (1979)
The Bard Owl (1980)
Apex of the Earth's Way (1984)
Skywriting (1988)
Drunk on a Glacier, Talking to Flies (1988)
Red Bracelets (1993)
The Road to Your House Is a Mountain Road (1995)
Mad Dogs of Trieste: New & Selected Poems (2000)
To You on the Other Side of This: Italian Translations (2000)
Nell'era delle cavallette / In the Age of Grasshoppers (2002)
The Green Piano (2005)

PROSE

Island of the Sun (1991)
Threading the Maze (1992)
Tracking the Serpent: Journeys to Four Continents (1997)
The Walker (2003)

Janine Pommy Vega

The Green Piano

POEMS

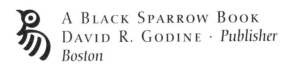
A Black Sparrow Book
David R. Godine · *Publisher*
Boston

This is
A Black Sparrow Book
published in 2005 by
David R. Godine, Publisher
Post Office Box 450
Jaffrey, New Hampshire 03452
www.blacksparrowbooks.com

The Black Sparrow Books pressmark is by Julian Waters
www.waterslettering.com

Frontispiece by Carol Zaloom
Book design and composition by Carl W. Scarbrough

LIBRARY OF CONGRESS
CATALOGING-IN-PUBLICATION DATA

Vega, Janine Pommy.
The green piano : poems / by Janine Pommy Vega.– 1st ed.
    p.   cm.
"A Black Sparrow book."
ISBN 1-57423-207-X (pbk. : alk. paper)
I. Title.
PS3566.O58G74   2005
811'.54–dc22
2005003643

First Edition
PRINTED IN CANADA

For my friends
in the Harvest Moon Collective

Contents

Note

In 1977, in upstate New York, I was walking up a steep snowy hill in the dark and saw a great display of the Geminids, a meteor shower. As I stood taking it in, it seemed I was watching some kind of music. *As though a chord were struck/ and one saw it, green/ some vast piano*, is how I described it in a poem.

Twenty years later, after giving a reading outside Florence, Italy, an art collector said he wanted me to paint a piano for him, for his collection of art done by poets. I remembered the piano on the hill, and said yes. The following year, when I returned to Florence on a performance tour of Germany and Italy, I brought the materials I would need to paint the piano: a star map, and photos of the aurora borealis and of meteor showers. The art collector provided me with a studio and two helpers. I painted the old upright he gave me a deep green, except for the back, which I painted a navy blue covered with transparent curtains of light, like the aurora borealis. The back was north. In the southern sky, under the keyboard and down by the pedals, I painted Orion and Sirius. Over the top and down the sides I painted the signs of the zodiac, with Gemini top center; arcing down the piano from that point were the meteors, which I painted with silver and gold sparkles. Under the keyboard cover I pasted a typed-out copy of my Geminids poem.

A few nights later, while on tour with poets from around the world and a handful of Italian musicians, I was sitting at table amid the usual hubbub of conversations, clinking glasses, the occasional song, when suddenly a hush fell. I looked across at the didgeridoo player, who in his day job was an astrophysicist. I said, "When everything gets quiet like that, as though the sky has come down to visit, I think of it as the green piano. Someone has lifted the lid and begun to play."

"Oh, absolutely," said the astrophysicist. "No question about it. The green piano."

That's how this book got its name.

Acknowledgments

Thanks to the editors and publishers of the following books, anthologies, and periodicals, in which some of these poems first appeared:

Across the Table, with Italian translation, by Janine Pommy Vega (accordion booklet, Longhouse, Guilford, Vermont); *Mean Ol' Badger Blues*, by Janine Pommy Vega ("Love Thy Poet" post-card series No. 28, Longhouse); *Nell'era delle cavallette / In the Age of Grasshoppers*, by Janine Pommy Vega (bi-lingual chapbook, Casa della Poesia, Salerno); *To You on the Other Side of This*, by Janine Pommy Vega (bi-lingual chapbook, City Lights Italia, Florence);

Celestial Graffiti, collected by Ira Cohen (The Ira Cohen Akashic Project, New York); *An Eye for an Eye Makes the Whole World Blind: Poets on 9/11*, edited by Allen Cohen and Clive Matson (Regent Press, Oakland); *Heart to Heart: New Poems Inspired by Twentieth-Century American Art*, edited by Jan Greenberg (Harry N. Abrams, New York); *Off the Cuffs: Poems by and about the Police*, edited by Jackie Sheeler (Soft Skull Press, Brooklyn); *Poems for the Nation: A Collection of Contemporary Political Poems*, edited by Allen Ginsberg with Eliot Kutz and Andy Clausen (Seven Stories Press, New York); *Poems from Penny Lane*, edited by Gary Parish Jr. and LeAnn Bifoss (Farfalla Press, Boulder); *Present/Tense: Poets in the World*, edited by Mark Pawlak (Hanging Loose Press, Brooklyn); *Shamanic Warriors Now Poets: An Anthology*, edited by J. N. Reilly and Ira Cohen (R & R Books, Glasgow); *Waging Words for Peace: Buffalo Poets Against War*, edited by Charles Culhane (Niagara River Press, Buffalo);

Arts for Peace; *Beat Scene*; *Booglit*; *The Butcher's Block*; *The Café Review*; *Counterpunch*; *Earth's Daughters*; *Ecstatic Yod*; *The Fool*; *Foolscap* (broadside periodical, England); *Hanging Loose*; *Home Planet News*; *House Organ*; *Hunger Magazine*; *Journal des Poètes* (Belgium/France); *JVC Books*; *Long Shot*; *Longhouse*; *Outlaw Magazine* (Wales); *Der Sanitäter* (Allen Ginsberg Homage, in German); *Transit*.

I would also like to thank the Golda Foundation for the grant that allowed me time to work on the manuscript of this book.

Blind Numbers over the Hill

Four Days before Rumi Died

for the Harvest Moon Collective,
in memory of Fielding Dawson

I could travel around the world
sending you postcards:
Nope.
These people are not as free
as you, either,
but the law does not allow postcards.

I could call you from across the country:
I had a dream! You were in it!
but there is no phone line
to a bank of cells,
just the telegram of a sixth sense
set precisely in the present.

Like Aymara natives of Lake Titicaca
for whom the moment of sundown is always
five o'clock, there's no time
for egos, yours or mine
they are luxuries in a prison
it's five o'clock, the sun is going down.

Realists in the best sense
you stretch out to embrace a word:
freedom, for instance
more than a sound, the thing itself
like love reverberating with all the tremors
of intimacy.

No one in prison presents a poem stoop shouldered
drowned in the rectitude of truth, romance
flies out the window,

the heart recognizes freedom
in an emissary from a distant place
in a lost tribesman from the human race.

In the workshop of diligent hammers
we send up
smoke signals,
some disappear
some messages have been caught from far away.

We gulp down freedom
like a cat with a canary in our stomach,
guards suspicious of smiles
look at me perplexed:
Where is that sound coming from?

Your open mic poems celebrate
what few in the life outside allow
Like a denizen of the Twilight Zone
I hop back and forth across a mirror
What is that singing in your belly?

the guards demand. What is that singing?
Because they don't know
I can't tell them
Just a telegram, I say,
a singing telegram from my next of kin.

Eastern Correctional Facility,
Napanoch, New York, December 13, 2001

The Tray

In the photo
someone comes through a doorway
it might be my mother, maybe me
locked away behind walls
behind walls
behind
walls
watching the snow

The person carries a tray
of objects, the photo is just a negative
indistinct, but they look
like hand–sized
ewers
What is she doing?
Is the act of bringing
a celebration, a signal to the world
that the pitchers are filled?

What they hold does not matter
as much as going through the door,
that time to this,
the sun dagger in the palm
of your hand, an unknown road
Will the pavement cave in?
Is there quicksand? Has a bridge collapsed?
I have something here to share with you
it has brought me to your door.

Eastern C.F., Napanoch, New York,
September 2000

C.O.

For someone like me, not born in Vermont
I don't build stone walls, I don't service the skiers,
I paint. I have since sixteen—
learned from the old-timers when I started
with nothing.
I'm fast, I'm clean, I work long hours
you have to to stay in this business.
Give me a solid-built New England farmhouse
I'll restore it to beauty it had in its youth;
the gables the trim the gaunt weathered siding
I have boxes of photos, before and after, for proof.

And I'm tall, I save hours on the ladder
with my reach, and I'm strong
I go sun-up to sundown,
you have to keep ahead of the shadows of winter,
keep one jump ahead of the snow.
All my gear in the panel truck, the lettering mine:
SCOTT MILLER PAINTS. Yes, I do.
Word spreads when you're as good as I am,
my name is my payroll
my health insurance and retirement fund.

But take this past winter, my wife and a kid,
two bright dry days between October
and April, the kitchens ran out
the Dairy Queen ceilings, the basement
renovations, we still have to eat.
A state job is the best you can hope for.
My name on that list for two solid years,
when it hit, it was my army time that brought
the job home: Correctional Officer
in Saint J.'s, the medium-security state prison.

From detailing windows I'm counting heads
every half hour now, my logbook entries
what I do for the paycheck—regular, thank God—
the coin of my realm a compassion I am
trying to keep. But some of these guys,
I don't envy their choices. I'll have
two years before I can transfer out.
This place could use a real scrape and paint job!
My rounds at night, the sleep check, the cigarettes
one after the other, their bodies sprawled out,
I'm locked in, too.

Willow, New York, December 1999

Christmas at Woodbourne

Sodden cardboard manger
at the front gate
to Woodbourne Prison
shrouded hills, lone gull's
screech atop the searchlight

Who says we are separate
from what we love?
Ramakrishna
would call that ignorance
Separate voices, separate

troubles, separate cells—
connectedness is
inseparable
from the consistency
of grace.

Woodbourne C.F., Woodbourne, New York,
December 1996

Offhand, from a Word

Wide open, sag mother,
refulgent among churches,
is it a sin to sweep Apollo under the rug?
A sin to carry a temple in your pocket?

There's a kind of lie where we
don't exactly say, Who wants this war?
but bury it in letters, like a gangster
dumping cement overshoes in a lake.

Is the answer out in stars lurking
at the edge
juggling love with loss
black hole with radiant cradle?

Hansel and Gretel, the skeletal duo
knock on a door, their garish grins
offset by Easter bonnets.
Come in, come in,

the train is on fire, we fired
at everything and hit nothing,
desire unappeased raised
tiny flags

and they bound us
hand and foot
to the literal lateral
ladder on the roof.

Eastern C.F., Napanoch, New York,
December 1999

Patrick Nolan

I read your poems of childhood
how you were clipped cuffed routinely abused
by a stepfather who hated your bright red
hair, you hid it under a hat
he took your hat and threw it out
the car window

I thought of the Death Row inhabitants
how to a man and woman they were all
abused as children—the killers, rapists: 100%—
how the acorn doesn't fall far from the tree
how cruelty is a learned maneuver,
not a natural act

I stood up for your poems in the contest:
stark and exacting details
without self-pity, so a reader was
moved to tears, and you won third prize.
I went to see you, like visiting a foreign
country in the Sacramento floods

All the workshops at Folsom cancelled
due to rain, they gave me a room off the Yard
with only two students, you and another
as though I'd come to see you in Turkey
we had a one-hour private audience
your bright red hair dark with years inside

A frog started piping near the drain in a corner
you stopped our meeting to find him
and took him out, gave him a chance

at survival. I thought how compassion
starts with oneself to include all others,
how your poems and you have transmuted

Last night I heard you died.
I've just come down the mountain
I studied the bare trees in the sun, they said
you knew it was coming, there were hundreds
of maple blossoms on the forest floor
some reds are naturally beautiful.

Willow, New York, April 14, 2000

Photograph

The brush strokes defining
roads, rooftops, harvest, cloudy sky
How can a camera delineate distance?

Is it time to step into
another dimension, a step where the foot
out in the air hooks onto an unseen shoulder of land?

Can a camera do this?
Could a young girl who never shot a photo show us?
How could she know?

The mountain stands leafless over a highway
shoulders ridgelines slopes defined by trees,
discreet cross–hatchings to the naked eye

She walks in a city. How would she see it?
In the shadow of new leaves on the sidewalk?
In the sag of warehouses at the pier?

The eye is not a camera
The camera is not a brush
An opening suggests itself

in the bars of a playground
shadowed on pavement
littered with tiny white blossoms.

Eastern C.F., Napanoch, New York,
December 14, 2000

Going into a Wishbone

We jumped the stile
and landed in brittle grass
the trees were drumheads
in the intermittent wind
we knew, even if we didn't say,
the thin song swallowing up our shadows
and the edges we left behind.

Walking along the dry clay road
our callused feet tap tapping
the yawning gulf, the egg–shaped hole
there was nothing you could give to make us
promise we wouldn't dance
one day we wouldn't
dance one day.

Eastern C. F., Napanoch, New York,
January 10, 2000

Blind Numbers over the Hill

for Bob Hausrath

I

In the vestibule of a prison
civilians I've indicted to myself surprise me
speaking of the woods, how beautiful in summer,
"I could spend my whole life in there."
A woman reflected in lobby window
walks ghostlike into the trees

The hunters, gatherers, farmers, woodsmen
circumscribed by diminishing land and loss
of jobs are the new jacks
a great rushing in at ten to eight
like the door on a factory morning

"48% of prisoners who leave come back,"
he says, "but only 24% of the college grads do."
Up a hill at the side of the road, hidden by
blackberry canes from traffic
is Attica's graveyard

A century of numbers marches
over the hill on uniform headstones
13987, 5677, 3429
In 1982, eleven years after the Attica uprising
they started putting in names

A grasshopper over V Cruz, 98G0370
outside the walls
in the earth who knows him
by feel, touch, grace of laughter
and rage of fists

14

12306 was someone
who laughed wept sickened and died
2342 the crickets are singing 1357
300 regulation tombstones
stand by the highway in the hot autumn sun

Like a war fought inside
another country, armed men exacting
revenge against poverty violence drugs
the same seven neighborhoods
illiteracy, despair, O unforgiving nation!

19924, 911090, no year no born no died
no name—forbidden perhaps
to carve the name. The later ones
with dates tell us they didn't live long:
age 48, 37, 41. Was it AIDS?

Were the first ones buried in common graves?
The AIDS patients in disaster bags?
5154, 5677, ancient maples
witness the unholy commerce:
dig up the earth, put in the numbers

Like the old–time cash register receipts
told you not what item but
how much you paid
23B481, 22717
cabbage moths, red–fruited sumac

Someone regularly mows the lawn
military style like the Arlington
Here's R. Morin, on staff
at the college, who seriously proposed
to at least one woman every day

No praise or blame
the shame of a village
blind numbers over the hill.

II

In the last hundred years or so
Sally Cunningham died,
all we know is she
was epileptic, lived and died behind
asylum walls, the original Shaker village
and was more than likely sterilized
Miss Sally Cunningham

A thousand graves in soldierly precision
dot the field behind the Shaker house
mowed by a prisoner
of the medium–secure prison
that has festooned stone walls with razor wire
and locked in two thousand men

No birth or death for Miss Cunningham
or for Robert McGee
no personal accomplishments.
"You broke down, Ma'am?"
The prison guard I knew would come
peers in my car window.

"This was the epileptics' graveyard,
wasn't it? Sure are a lot of tombstones.
Imagine walling someone up for epilepsy."

"Well, you know those days," he drums
on his temple, "if you weren't perfect,
they locked you away."

       III

In a wide fertile valley in rosy autumn
in the field behind the historic poorhouse
headstones have settled crookedly
in the weedy graveyard

Most of the twenty stones are blank
no name no number no born no died
here lies someone too much trouble
to record, someone poor

Wyoming & Livingston Counties, New York,
September 2000

From *A Week of Kindness*

She stops on a dime
a plate of pigeon eggs arrests her flight
she is bound for the drawing room
the cozy fire and cockscomb of continuous wing

antlers grow from the naked brain
the hat on fire, the song of victory
in an empty mirror,
I saw a man

portray a chicken once
funniest thing I'd ever seen
his neck
jerked forward, pecking the air

it works as a mnemonic
device, a triangle of moving hands
you hawk offstage into the wind
and a hen steps up for her morning meal

it is you the chicken
the sun coming up on Tibetan plateau
the iron dagger, a blue green
flash on the winter snow.

Eastern C.F., Napanoch, New York, Spring 2000

Please Look Both Ways before Crossing

The Desert Storm we raised in Iraq
     was a terrorist act. We called it retaliation.
     The killing of tens of thousands of teenagers
     dressed as soldiers was, we said, a casualty of war.

We tried out the marvelous flares and bombs
     and watched the pyrotechnics safely six thousand miles
     from the action in privileged seats. Six days of televised
          spectaculars.
     We made bull's eyes with Saddam Hussein at the center.
     He's a bully, we said. He has to come down.

The invasion of Grenada was a terrorist act.
     We did not like the island president speaking
     so loudly about his brand of socialism
     so close to our door.

To threaten invasion of Colombia, Peru, Bolivia
     because they insist on tending the coca Yaguar Huaca
     gave them to withstand tiredness, hunger, thirst, and cold,
     and that we insist on buying and selling
     is a terrorist act
     no less than Sendero Luminoso's gouging the eyes out
     of CIA agents, and leaving the bodies in fires on a hill.

Acts of terrorism hurt people. Blow up bridges, skyscrapers,
     hospitals, villages, naval fleets, schools, places of worship,
     and you will hurt people.

Please look both ways before crossing.
     We export principally garbage and weapons of war,
     we stay well fleshed on the work of others.
     Flexing the military capitalist muscle, the "My God
     is bigger than your God" muscle, will not bring us home.

Women know it. We dress the dead. We sweep up
       the mess, we make our way back to the fields
       and re-plant. We put food on the table, we survive.
       Modesty is not such a bad hat. It's certainly lighter
       than armor, and cheaper to care for.

"Are you locked down?" the ABC newsman asked
               Governor Pataki
       after the Twin Towers shattered. A jailhouse term,
       invented by jailers for locking all cells when
               trouble strikes.
       In the air bristling with fear and hate, are we
               locked down?

Are we safely back in our cells, accepting partial information
               as fact,
       believing the president will punish the guilty, forgetting
       it was our CIA who trained Osama bin Laden in the 80s
       and our arms dealers who backed Hussein? Are we
               locked down?

Please look both ways.
       The genuine desire for peace and freedom
       held in the heart of American hearts
       is the same in every heart in the world. It does not require
       victory, empire, subjugation, retaliation, or arrogance.
       It will not survive there.

The thousands buried as the Twin Towers crumbled,
               the heroism
       of ordinary people, the selfless service of hundreds of
               firemen,
       policemen, rescue workers, the enormity of their sacrifice,

let them stand for this: that we live in one world,
    a small one
to hold all the souls we are today,
and any striking out will hurt more people.

America, please look both ways.
    We can't point everywhere with blame and forget
    ourselves. Terrorist acts, like the pigeons on tenement
    rooftops, the sport of kings on the Lower East Side,
    always come home to roost.

Mount Morris, New York, September 12, 2001

The Smile

Then you watch the wolves
herd up to eat and sleep:
    the unmistakable order,
    the alpha male with
exaggerated prowess. The

smile of his sidekick as he sidles up
    has nothing to do with mirth,
    no bridge between equals, but a
moat separating one role from another.

In the castle habitat, every role
    is integral to survival: the mother,
    the cubs, and babysitting Uncle Irving, who
lets the kids walk over him, and nip his
ears, and chase his tail. He cuffs them into line
    only when he has to, doing it
    with an easy smile.

Soledad, California, January 1998

In the Age of Grasshoppers

A grasshopper with a roomy apartment
building for a stomach
tiptoes around the edge of the world
It would take forty billion dollars to feed, clothe,
provide good water and sewerage systems,
basic education and medical care
for every man, woman and child in the world.

The grasshopper army on its hind legs
looks like a grinning radiator grill
320 billion for defense, 100 billion for a war
no one wants against a beautiful land
and its ancient people—first Afghanistan, now Iraq,
bin Ladens and Bushes in the Carlyle Group
turning hefty profits for the last twenty years.

You never heard grasshoppers devour a field?
You never heard the crackling of houses
split like matchsticks, children
with swollen bellies and big eyes
looking at you when the crops go down?
Have you heard the whining language of insects
eating until no one is left and nothing standing?

But they always leave a little, don't they?
A little left over to work the machine
through the plague of locusts, the rain of blood.
In the age of miracles a doctor weeps
as he recounts the marvelous plastic surgery
he was asked to undo on an insect woman
without a mouth. They had sewed her lips shut,
layer by layer, and left a small round hole

for a straw, so she could eat, left a monster
as a living example to the others. The doctor wept
at the healing art perverted to instill raw terror.
Scratch any insect in the Carlyle Group
see if blood comes out
or is it ancient dust, the bones of bloodsuckers
radiator teeth chewing arms and legs
like garbage compacters because they can't stop eating
because we let them, because they can.

> *Eastern C.F., Napanoch, New York,*
> *January 24, 2002*

Driving While Black

Daily News clipping, August 20, 1998

Jawad Abdullah left his native
Trinidad in the 1970s
never suspecting his dark skin
and long dreadlocks
might pose an arresting problem

He now thinks they attract the attention
of police
who have stopped and searched him
more than a dozen times
since 1974

He's been mostly cited for minor
infractions, but Abdullah's
anger grows—
largely because it is difficult to prove
as he and others suspect
that such stops result from racial bias

The ability to prove bias
could change
if a so-called Driving While Black
Bill before the U.S. Senate
passes in the coming weeks.
It would require the attorney general's
office to collect data on traffic stops
and searches, to show patterns

Police
largely
oppose the bill

insisting it would
create an undue burden
on law enforcement officers
and wouldn't necessarily prove a thing.

Eastern C.F., Napanoch, New York, August 1998

Business on the Hill, as Usual

with special thanks to William Blake and
Helen Caldicott

Behind the cross three Roman soldiers are throwing dice
their lives illuminated by the game
the fourth guard holding the spears peers at them
playing for remnants of somebody's clothes
if it's true what they say, they could make a killing:
business as usual on the hill.
The dairy farmer tries to survive the glut of agribusiness
by swelling his livestock to two thousand cows, herded
single file to the milking machines, once they start
milking they never go out. Thirteen to fifteen
years through the tunnel back to the barn
no outside
no luminous green
the game will brook no interruption.

Look at their eyes.
Once in a while a cow escapes, the man says,
jumps the fence, otherwise
they live in the barn
looking through the screen at the fall of evening.
Now the people at the cross look up,
it's getting dark out,
everyone here knows it doesn't have to
be like this, even if we say nothing.
What about the nuclear bombs like tidy eggs
in the psyches of men in Washington?
What about the pathological disregard
for consequences? Twenty thousand dead
in Afghanistan, a direct result of our war.
How many more in Iraq?

In the central cage of a prison
four men sit in a box, three guards outside
are eating ice cream, one guard measures out chains
to cuff and ankle each prisoner leaving the cage.
"Tuck your shirt in!" he says.
It's business as usual.
"What flavor ice cream you got?" asks the guard
with the big gut, leaning against the bars,
and we're all in jail
those of us in the box, those of us with the jobs
the dice game has consumed us all
we drink the milk of imprisoned cows.

How can witnesses be said to foster terrorism?
The psyches of men who sleep with bombs
before the test drop
cradle the babies in simulacra of radiant birth—
where are the onlookers this night?
How can we heal the men with birth pangs
for dead eggs, the believers in controlled nuclear strikes,
the herding in of the field of dreams
the thumbs up sign for ownership?

How can we re-seed the fields,
let the cows out, redolent with summer haze
and their own good nature?
How can we take apart the premise,
pull the nails out,
pull the Bastille down, plant the open market space,
watch the redwing blackbirds and think about nothing?
How can we create the grace of freedom?

Eastern C.F., Napanoch, New York, June 2002

For Boats Only

April is the month to bring the boats down
    to the river.
The Thirteenth Amendment to the U.S. Constitution
    says slavery shall not exist, except as punishment
    for a crime for which a person will have been convicted.
The geese are coming north again, they settle in marshes
    on both sides of the river, hunters wait
    for dawn behind the duck blinds.
The river town has 5000 souls. Two prisons bring the official
    count to nearly 8 thou. Most inmates work for Corcraft,
    the prison industry; they earn a dollar a day. That brings
    the total income down, the town qualifies for
        federal funds.
Renewal projects are everywhere, refurbished two–story
    brick buildings haven't looked this good since 1905.

The cruelest shots in the schoolyard are reserved for
        the fat kids,
    the ones now lumbering down the launching ramp
        behind
    overweight moms and overweight dads
    in fat pickups and SUVs, tugging fatter boats.
A roly–poly parade in the working–class town.
    Correctional officers and families. The big boats groan
    down cement ramps and enter the water.
The State Rep is ecstatic. State taxes pay for the prisons.
    They employ more people than cement plants
        farther north.
    C.O.s never get laid off. It's a cash cow.
Taxation without representation: the prisoners can't vote,
    and the townspeople elect a rep who favors more prisons.

Corcraft soap in all state universities, Corcraft planters
    at thruway toll booths, Corcraft license plates on all
        New York cars,
    Corcraft dog tags for every doggie,
Corcraft crews remove asbestos from all state prisons,
        the Motor Vehicle
    Department phones are manned—rather womened—
        by prisoners,
    Corcraft drapes and furniture in all state offices,
        Corcraft beds
    in every prison and reform school.
Like the robust arches of the salt cathedral dug out by hand
            by native
    slaves in Zipaquirá, the salt mine outside Bogotá,
        Colombia,
the glorious New York infrastructure is held up for next
        to nothing—
    only sixteen cents an hour, twenty-one cents at the best.

By May and June the river will roar with Evinrude engines,
    the fat kids will carry down hefty coolers of sandwiches
    and Coca-Cola, everyone will get aboard
And ain't life grand?

Willow, New York, January 30, 2003

400 to 21 Against Megadeath Media Takeover

The e-mails have been buzzing for months:
constituent opposition to the fat cats disguised
as aerobically trim millionaires in business suits,
Michael Powell leading the parade,
was one last shot we had before the media rip-off.
It's already crystal clear air play programming
coast to coast—no blues, no jazz, no real country—
musicians themselves tell you they don't listen,
and the big guys want to chomp down more—
more air time glub more newspapers glub glub
Hitler had it there in *Mein Kampf*:
Say it enough times, and they will believe you.
Own enough radio stations, enough TV stations,
all the newspapers, who's to say no?
Stalin got that, too.
Who's to know it's any other way but how we paint it?
So people spoke up, they rattled the phones of the
House of Reps, and the House voted 400 to 21
against the FCC proposal that private corporations
could own more public air space.
The Federal *Communications* Commission,
a misnomer like Green Haven, Albion,
Great Meadows and Grove Land—bucolic prisons all,
Federal Anti-communications Commission spells FAC
like FAC the people's airways and lifeblood of democracy!
Plugged and clogged as it is, we're still here breathing,
we don't want to be quiet.
The Christian zealots, the Civil Rights leaders,
the Writers Guild, Consumers Union—
unlikely bedfellows—agree on this:
We don't want to go dumbly down to slaughter
we want to speak up.

Give us a radio dish, we want to sing.
We want to clap hands and dance, wake up a nation,
one sleeping citizen at a time.
The aerobic gentlemen in the million–dollar suits
are up–front about it: "We need consolidation for the *money*.
We need to pay for the Super Bowl!"
Fascism dressed in the lily lamb's wool of capital,
O you poor things!
Computer keys are clicking in the background:
It ain't over till the fat lady sings,
and if she sings, when we hear it.

Eastern C.F., Napanoch, New York, July 27, 2003

Habeas Corpus Blues

for SRR, CG, BH, CP, CC & LJP, warriors all

Habeas corpus? Habeas corpus?
700 years built into that question. Have you got the body?
A cornerstone of justice: Can you show
a body for the people to see?
In police investigations, in the kidnapping of foreign citizens
for U.S. international terrorism,
in the prison system holding up our economy as surely
as slavery in the early days,
in the rubbery tentacles of parole
that can reel a body back in years after release
for a dirty urine, for an in–your–face political stance, for a rally,
for a public speech
they can reel you in like so many lobster traps
in the Gulf of Maine, reel you into the Deuce Club
where you live your years out two at a time,
parole denied, and parole denied, as long as they have
domain over the body. Habeas corpus?

Yes they have the body. And they can gnaw away at anyone
on the outside who tries to get in. I've calculated
in ten thousand days, more than twenty–six years,
I've seen prisoners ganged up on by guards with sticks
right in front of me, an ordinary citizen, their glasses
broken at the Visiting Room door, I've seen
lines of men with carbon–copy shackles
from the slave days shuffle by me, have seen whole
families reviled for visiting, mothers stripped
of underwire bras and dignity. I have worked inside
a prison for women forbidden to touch, forbidden
to hug each other. I have been in meeting rooms
wired for sound that could kill the inner ear

and provoke waves of nausea. I've been hustled through
the back way to sidestep the murder
of a man in solitary. What can they do?
Anything they want. They have the body.

Habeas corpus blues for Blue,
the poet who will never get out under Governor Gray.
Not one murderer released on his watch, he overrode
his own investigative panels, his own California judges.
Habeas corpus blues for every longtermer who has violence
in his particular crime in Pataki's New York: only one out of
seventeen released by Parole Board, Robespierre's cabal
of commissioners—twenty-two people who sit in judgment
over seventy-two thousand souls.
Habeas corpus blues for an Irish warrior, Gary McGivern
wheeled on the gurney to his deathbed, who would not
release his grip on his sister's hand, would not
let them take him down.

Habeas corpus blues for a system
I wish I could hang from the nearest tree, but overthrow
is molecular, from the inside out.
Lenore Kandel says irony is the fulcrum
of the universe, these are gray green smothering times,
cowardice is king.
Christ is more alive in some of these men, said
the chaplain of Attica, than most of the passersby outside.
Habeas corpus blues for a citizenry
that does not see if they come for me tonight
it's for you in the morning, for a press
that won't speak out, will not bear witness.

Habeas corpus? Do they have the body
in the body politic?
Mmm hmm.
It looks like every day they have a little bit more.

Willow, New York, January 15, 2003

Wartime Kitchen

I think of Yannis Ritsos's women
marching to the kitchen at the first sound of war
I think of the bulk of Grandma in Jersey City,
a bulk I could never duplicate as I pad across
the floor to grind the sweet basil grown
last season, to brush the cat, to chop garlic
for salad dressing

Deliberately quiet tasks, though I could start
throwing pots around like my mother, I can tell you,
make such a ruckus you would wonder who had
gone insane, and it's the world
in the photos I will not bring home,
in the leering sneering posture of an imposter
president, put in charge by corporate fists

I could show you how weeping has worn a hole
in my heart as deep as the slippers
she thrust her feet in cold Polish mornings,
I've become that babushka woman
witnessing carnage, all wisecracks are out
of place, no jokes for broken children or screaming
mothers, dead soldiers are children themselves

No jokes for the children, everybody's children
I do not forgive their slaughter
the oil the arms the gold piled high as this house
cannot buy their laughter, cannot bury their shrieks
in the night, I accuse the old white men drowned in greed
of their murder, I will bang every pot and pan
I own for a world free from their hands.

Willow, New York, April 2003

Memo for Memorial Day:
Tillman Likely Killed by Friendly Fire

Associated Press article in Kingston (N.Y.) Freeman,
May 30, 2004

Former NFL defensive back
Pat Tillman, 27, walked away from
a $3.6 million contract with the Arizona
Cardinals to join the Army
following the Sept. 11, 2001, attacks.

According to Army investigations,
Tillman was shot to death April 22
after a friendly Afghan soldier in Tillman's unit
was fired upon,
and other U.S. soldiers then fired
in the same direction.

But an Afghan military officer
told the A.P. on Saturday
that Tillman died because of a
"misunderstanding,"
when two mixed groups of American
and Afghan soldiers began firing wildly
in the confusion following
a land mine explosion.
Speaking on condition of anonymity,
the Afghan official said,
"There were no enemy forces present
when Tillman died."

At Fort Bragg, an officer
with the 30th Engineer Battalion said
the circumstances of Tillman's death
do not change his heroism.

37

"A lot of us sacrifice something, but
 no one sacrificed as much as he did to join,"
Sgt. Matt Harbursky said,
 as he prepared
 to play a round of golf at the base course.
"And it really doesn't matter how he
 was killed, it's sad."

Willow, New York, May 31, 2004

Animal Kingdom

You speak of the wolf, the owl, the vixen
I see a woman going to East 10th Street
not combing the bar exactly
but standing in her body, come what may

On the pillow next to her in the morning
was something she wished she had not
dragged home, the pockets of desire
spilled out into aggression
the man with the face not entirely set in its bones
took to leaving her obscene messages
she remembered his skin in the dark
like something drowned

The bald hightops of another man
who suggested bondage, suggested
letting him tie her up
the logical outcome a loop turned back
upon itself, men women and scorpions
the only ones who can poison themselves,
leaving no one shining in the parlor

The fat man with pigskin gloves
in hundred–degree summer New York City,
his porcine face shopped for porno photos,
always ready to meet one of the girls,
desire spilling out of hot pockets, caught
in the loop, the same tin fantasy, a fish
flopping out on the ice at the hole in a lake

In the woods the wolf wakes up:
Salt peanuts! Salt peanuts! a robin singing
at 5 A.M. The wolf unravels herself
from her warm lair, lopes in easy strides
to the river, and drinks.

Eastern C.F., Napanoch, New York, May 2004

Inanna Is Singing Us to Sleep

The Green Piano: I

When silence falls
in the dining room
it's the green piano:
someone has lifted the lid
and begun to play.

Consciousness of a face
one's face
brings melancholy
like the cup one hates, the contents
of which are separation.

When I return
you'll be going away
let's take a walk, hold hands
remember what it was first
held us close, good–humored
happy like this.

Pistoia, November 30, 2001

"We're just lucky"

you said. It was spring,
I was out in the garden with the phone
you were in your Chelsea Hotel room,
we were talking about how long
we'd loved each other
"My whole adult life," I said, almost
thirty-eight years, and
I looked around the garden at the flowers.
You had given me my last time down
a little black vase
"And what will I do with this?" I said.
"I'll have to schlepp it around all day,
why don't you just give me a handkerchief?"
"Take it," you said, "I might not be here
when you come back."

And you might not see the flowers.
I started taking photos of each week's blossom
inside your vase up on a red table in the sun
brought the roll to your hospital bed,
but you couldn't see them

My exasperation at your pretzel shape
some days, your limbs twisted around
each other
deep in your coke run
exaggerated grimaces and skeletal frame
grasping the five bucks that would get you
straight in the morning

Your exasperation at my recently
straight persona: no smoke no drugs no wine no beer
much less of a context for talk, except
for the wide view
over thirty–eight years, how lucky

Willow, New York, May 22, 2002

Love from a Distance

How many years has it been? Four?
    Are you looking at your stomach sideways
    in the mirror, saying,
    "Pretty good for my age, hunh?"

I have trouble seeing you
    in this garden, trouble imagining you
    crossing the border, a wild card in the salsa bands
    of Spanish Harlem

You're looking through the reading glasses you hate to wear
    at a schedule for the last bus to Kingston
    from New York City. At 11:30? When the clubs are just
    getting started? You'd prefer to see dawn over city streets.

What I can see is the laughter
    doing your version of Cantinflas
    for a room full of Anglos who don't know
    who that is or who you are or what you're saying

What translates is the largesse of a man
    who doesn't comprehend the language
    never will
    and can make them laugh nonetheless.

Eastern C.F., Napanoch, New York, March 1997

Heart

Across an arena of floorboards
light arrives
not summoned
light arrives on its own

a choreography of muscles
pulling the sea to pieces
in subterranean passageways
surf rolls over the stones

electrical pulse in a nest
of wings, the folded heron
awaits the large arrival of the sun
rose petals on your lower lip

heart in its conjugal feast
a fist milking the cow of pleasure
Inanna is singing us to sleep
in the corral:

Visit me as you would a holy country
where the good crops grow as promised
and the separate thrones resemble
the waves of the sea.

Eastern C.F., Napanoch, New York, Spring 1999

Withdrawal

The silence billows out and in
like curtains, childhood movies
on the bedroom wall, headlights coming down
Palisades Avenue turning the corner
project scenarios through the rustling lace.

Two men climb the stairs in the movie
narrow stairs in a sunny afternoon
it's my grandmother's house, they bring down
a coffin again and again. Sometimes a pail as well.
A slow determinate of destiny pulls

at the bed sheets.
Crickets cradle the stillness
bear paws clawing the air are drawn
like magnets to a birth of hands,
eyes laughing from an ordinary pillow.

The thick jellied soup
allows no movement, no stretch and pull
through Technicolor photographs
no collection of vegetables tumble through
September afternoon.

Flailing arms and urgent belly
head for the surface
the dry dock of uncertain capture
Nothing alive but wonder:
how quiet it can get after you've passed through.

Willow, New York, September 1998

Right Here

Ripples on the underbelly of a concrete bridge
sun on the moving stream
a heron takes flight
blue pterodactyl
from the center of town

Across the stream is an open field
tenacious spider
crosses my hand, a man crosses
the street with his dog
says this is a lovely place to sit

He's right.
I'm grateful you're alive
on the planet, that I got to know you,
that we're both here at the same time.
Amazing.

Rhinebeck, New York, September 1998

Garden

I've spent the day spring cleaning
dreaming of how I would
plant strawberries
Brussels sprouts, flowers that
bloom in succession
week after week, so your windows
would open every day into color

I've been checking the progress
of shoots
buds and flowers, looking
through leafless trees into space
I've walked a tangled line through the woods
where I'd build a fence, where I'd put the gates
and surround you with my joy.

Willow, New York, April 1999

50

Rivulet

Ice candles
like the backs of women
torso to calves

no sound as they break
into moving water, no bells
in a row along the branch

ice mittens
over leafy stone conglomerate
forest floor

singing rivulet
from spring-fed pool
at the foot of a maple

you will be my mother
hands in moss you will
be the one

who takes this body sings
my fears to sleep
you are the cradle and lullaby

ice fingers the color
of Indian pipes in rows
along the branches.

Tremper Mountain, New York, February 1999

Birch Fat

Old ritual of birch bark
taken for kindling
while the ground is dry

downed trunks
peeled for the white
chalky rings

in brittle cold
the beech buds
fattening

chickadee crow
and gatherer
quietly busy

a rivulet runs
alongside tar road
in shimmering sun

laughing like me
with my bundle
happy go

lucky
both of us
down the hill.

Tremper Mountain, New York, February 1999

Doing Nothing

Cathedral arch in the iris
reflected in sunglasses
here on the sidewalk
an absolutely ordinary piece of ground
the points of sun
in the pupil
march through lenses to the ridgeline
the little dog digs on the icy trail
and this is it
one of the hundred ways we have
to collect the light.

Tremper Mountain, New York, February 12, 2000

After Frost

Whose woods these are I think I know,
the beech copse rattling as I go,
pausing to notice from time to time
the blue white diamonds on the snow.

Blue green orange crystals shine
as I follow the deer tracks in a line
over shoulder and hillock, stump and stone
into silent dreams of the porcupine.

Gaining the ridgeline I stand alone
with the wind, a clatter of crows, and the drone
of airplanes trespassing overhead
while I contemplate like Thoreau what I own:

Deep sleep of the woods in her royal bed,
the snow unbroken like risen bread,
a quiet dropping inside the head
where songs are born and the soul is fed.

Mount Tremper, New York, February 2000

Telemeter

The instrument broadcasts
heartbeats
audible across the expanse

of space-ship hub
Recovery Room, monitoring
us hooked to the wall

Barry the vegetable produce man
Max the iron worker
and me

beeping in arrhythmic chorus
three ducks
hooked to the telly

beeps
like bullfrogs at the side
of a lake

a quiet
alien
conversation

three necks side by side
carotid bandages the O.R. nurse
calls the Tripartite

three
live tree frogs
in the dark spring night.

Benedictine Hospital, Kingston, New York,
March 14, 2000

55

Jerusalem Artichoke

I learned a hundred lessons
in the garden
dig
deeper was the first

the least little root
of Jerusalem artichoke
carries a sturdy new
plant into April

like the vaguest hope for
a friend
buried, like a sliver of moon
in the heart in spring

there are hundreds of sun chokes
take more than you need
give them to people you've
never seen

look for me
in the garden laughing
and crying at once.

Willow, New York, May 1999

Telling the Beads

I can't remember the name for
telling the beads
one by one they roll through
my fingers, left hand
right hand
each syllable a step
two steps
up the mountain

I don't remember when
I learned the freedom
of repeated
sounds
a stone dropped
into ripples widening
the sound a rope pulling
me up the mountain

Castaneda curled in his fingers
and crossed his eyes
so space rushed in
and ambushed the walker
One hundred and eight is four
twenty–sevens, beads on a string
sometimes I remember to count
sometimes I forget

The walls
separating one from oneness
disappear
like sugar in water

like sweat rolling off the side
of a face, the boundless
catches up and we are
empty in that joy.

Eastern C.F., Napanoch, New York, August 2000

The Other Side

She sat on the stoop all summer
spread out, a hill of flesh
folded quietly, crocheting
through hot afternoons, soft-spoken
Mrs. Lyden, her blue eyes
darting from 47th Street stickball
game to the doily in her hand
to firehouse tenement life.

Her oldest daughter Lily
was thirty-two, wore black
old-lady shoes, and carried groceries
home for my mother, a quarter a trip.
She worked for other women, too.
When she had enough, she went to the movies,
Colony Theater, didn't miss a day.
Kindly Mrs. Lyden one floor above us
with her pink face and lemon candy.

One night the alley exploded
into mean, sarcastic, deep-pitched barks
Who was sobbing? Not a child.
Whose voice was pleading?
Should we call the police?
Who was the strange attacker?
I looked at my sister, older than I.
Shhh, she whispered, that's Lily crying.
That's the other side of Mrs. Lyden.

Attica C.F., Attica, New York, March 2001

59

First

Aunt Sabina's apartment is always
messy, with comfortable clutter
my mother would never allow:
bright splashy fabric, big black
and white pillows,
the tasseled lamp, the deck of cards
on the coffee table, two glasses
still smelling of last night's rye, an ashtray
full of butts and stale air

Outside the rules I help myself
to morning orange juice
bare feet in nightgown on sticky floor
and Hey, he says,
my Uncle Boozie, chewing his tongue
Come here, he says, only him and me
He lifts up my nightgown, grabs my ass
wields an imaginary carving knife:
Let me get some of that ham!

Albion C.F., Albion, New York, March 2001

Ghost

Perhaps if she hadn't run into him
before she would've accepted
philosophically that the trunk lid
fell with her head inside,
hit her temple, gave her a nasty bump,
end of story.

But she lifted the trunk lid again
to make sure, the car parked
on steep snowy incline,
to see if gravity would pull it down.
It didn't. Like every other time, it stayed
up in the air, the lid stayed open.

She had met him before,
the homebound ghost, when he'd dropped
a screen onto the pillow where five minutes
before her head had lain, when the night light
had exploded four inches from her face.
Ice cubes on her forehead now

she kept an eye open as the moon sank,
stars set, kept the flickering candle lit
until she dropped off.
An earthquake violently
rocked her bed. Everything in her corner
of the world was wide awake.

Collins C.F., Western New York, March 2001

Portable Altar

A silk kerchief
candle incense bowl of water
burning stick on a tiny plate

in a motel room
the miniature world a focus
like the tiny owl marching over

a battlefield in a dream of war
eyes riveted to the fire
heart drawn

to a locus, a place to rest
inside constant travel,
a candle flickers

off earrings
photograph
wisp of smoke.

Wyoming C.F., Western New York, March 2001

Lily

A cotton blue-checked summer dress
perhaps a little too small for her body
muscles that scrubbed the immaculate floors
of their upstairs apartment, she did
the grunt work, her sturdy arms and legs lugged
groceries, twenty-five cents a bag
the buttonholes of her bodice stretched
by ample breasts

Grinning shyly in our kitchen
Is it a retarded trait to be willing
to laugh at yourself?
At least twice a month came the terrible
screams, the blows of her mother
her childlike wails, her Cinderella life
without the slippers, she trudged every day
after work to the movie, and grinned
at the screen when it came on

One rainy afternoon at the Colony
I came upon her by accident
her familiar checked dress, her heavy arm
on the plush velour seat, she was
grinning at the man beside her, sort of pudgy
who was grinning back
In the bleak dead-end frozen late Fifties
flickering gray gloom black-and-white
feature, Lily and her friend were
grinning at each other, holding hands.

Eastern C.F., Napanoch, New York, July 2001

63

The Poppy of Georgia O'Keeffe

In a carmine extravagance
the skirts of a Spanish dancer swirl
flamenco rhythms, castanets
exuberant dancer
drumming her heels on a wooden floor
staccato barks, deep intricate guitars
the energy pulsing up from the dark
surrounds and enters

The poppy is wide open
her petals curve
like the skirts of a mountain
filled with the morning sun
we climb
and reaching the pinnacle shout
like the flower
in strict discipline, in eloquent satori
in the wild grace of black and red.

Mount Morris, New York, September 1999

64

The Closet

In the room
stifling as it can get only in Florida
with the windows open or the windows closed
I looked at the sea of shoes
hundreds of shoes
you were always so profligate in your undying
love for yourself

That time you got knocked down
by a motorbike in Thailand,
got up
and immediately went to the jewelry shop
to buy yourself a diamond earring
"I was so amazed to be alive, you see.
My supreme good fortune!"

The good fortune to be born inside
your body you took for granted:
dozens of shirts in cotton
linen, silk
gorgeously tailored pants
extravagant tea gowns, peach
with flounces and rhinestones

Your son and I surveyed the closet
the overflowing drawers, the weighted shelves
cashmeres, leather jackets, gaudy
tropical shirts like so many
papagallos in Iquitos
without speaking about it we both
got dressed like you, and hit the streets.

Eastern C.F., Napanoch, New York, July 2002

Dialogue

Hey, are you sleeping?
    No.
Are you snoring with your eyes open?
    Are you making fun of a person with
    breathing problems?

How's your back?
    I think I have gas in my back.
Gas? What kind of gas?
    Gas from the belly. Somehow it gets trapped in the back.
Does that mean you fart from your wing bone?
    Ask your doctor. Every doctor knows about it.

Hey, I bought you something from the New Museum.
It's by another Belgian. The machine is 32 feet long,
called Cloaca—like the Roman sewer.
I must say it's not that pretty. Read the pamphlet.
It parrots the human digestive system.
At 2:30 every day the machine takes a shit.
    I don't need to read it.
    The man who made it
    is definitely not a Walloon. Must be a Flem.

So I make steamed veggies and brown rice,
you eat Kwik Mart tacos from a microwave.
I make oatmeal, you get a turkey sandwich on
white bread. That's what you ate before we met.
It's a skidder's diet!

Hey, the jacket looks good on you. It's not
the one I took to the cleaner. Which one is that?

    The skidder's jacket.

What?

Whirlpool sucking us down
swallowing sound
in the intricate maze of canals
the song is drowned
translated transmigrated
into a form we don't recognize.
When the words
came tiptoeing through space
I heard it my way:
bird, knife–blade
interrogation in a bare cell.
In the mirror it came
confused, the whereabouts
of its origin lost
in the frayed seams of an old coat
on a winter day coming out
of the movies.
What did you say to me?
What did you say?

Eastern C.F., Napanoch, New York, February 1, 2001

Skunk Valentine's Day

It's the skunk's birthday
or she's fallen in love and can't control herself
or she's found another way in and is having babies
under the house again, early this year,
or the cat in his role of alpha male
has ticked her off

It's easier sitting outside
than in when the gas seeps up
the blue gray stripes on the snow have covered
the shrinking snowgirl and her vanishing pinhead
Skunk Valentine's Day she keeps telling us,
as though even the air is all about her.
I'm glad you called.

Willow, New York, February 14, 2003

Feet

I look down at the flat feet by the toilet
my feet, this life

First we're hypnotized that this is it
then we're saying good–bye

How many nights have I done this?

Shivering moth wings on the screen
Outside hypnosis

it really is good–bye.

Willow, New York, August 12, 2001

Gregory

I

Clean-shaven, cleared away, like a baby
tucked in bed with undressed eyes
a cold drink from a deep well
to see you
first friend in early teenage years
in New York City, then
Paris, San Francisco, London
friend snatched back from the bony doorway

jewel at the heart of a room full
of people, rose on the pillow
I'm reading your poems again
twisty pronouncements, singing lines
words that float like birds on the water,
how much you've changed the language
and the premise of speech

How without hesitation, all these years
you've jumped in, not
testing the waters
but to see
if the waters were ready for you.

Horatio Street, New York City, August 17, 2000

II

Someone said your ashes should be scattered
over Shelley's grave, someone said
you wanted to be buried in Potter's Field

because nobody goes to see those folks
Irvyne says you're all together now, the whole crew:
you Jack Allen Huncke Neal
Jack Micheline Ray Bremser

You were the one
who brought me into that
circle of men
you were the one who gave up
your time, who shared
your readings, who insisted
I learn Roman history

You taught us the usage of *my*
as though everything of consequence
sprang first from the poet's lips,
calling Gilgamesh *Gil Baby*
calling Roger and Irvyne's apartment
my old neighborhood, calling
Allen *my Allen*, Andy *my Andy*.

I was planning to fly out
and see you, to stay at your house,
there were two modes
I knew you in: loving and ruthless,
we met in both camps
through years of bad boy sacred clown
shout–downs, dozens of readings

On Horatio Street surrounded by friends
you were glad of time left, I told you
the story of Fernando in Paris,

after his paintings were hung in Musée
de l'Homme, and you wildly disagreed
with one corner of the painting, how he
snuck in with a paint bucket and changed it.

At exactly the moment you died
I was mapping my flight
so perhaps
we *were* meeting, my messenger
at the gate, my mentor, my partner
in crime, my Gregory
my friend.

Willow, New York, January 18, 2001

Thoughts in the Morning

for Martin Matz & Gary McGivern

To wake up in the morning weeping
the arm bones are refined the flesh diminished
to wake in the morning with the news of a lifetime
reduced to a maxim: the only service is selfless service
the time is finite cut into blocks and maps of action
maquettes of houses hang from the elbows
complete floor plans accompanied by junk habits
welfare lines, debris of demolition
How forge a new way
if it's only the old with another face? Can ardor
flattened under years of repetition spring forth
possessed of the moment?

Sometimes I just don't want to hear another prison poem
buried under years and locked into convention
cut off from leaps over the edge
If you whittle it down, whittle it down
you wind up with a hairy toothpick
a throwaway
Resplendent next to the johnny pump
is the self with no more ties to cut
no more edges to flirt with, all mammalian ardor
transmuted into something else

In real life the tearing away has the sound
of ligaments ripping, a huge ungainly bird sails out
improbably from the broken nest, a blue heron
looks more lizard–like than ever
no sailing without that tearing loose
one mistakes the shudder of the giant bird
for a large bush rippling in the wind
on closer inspection, in the rustling leaves
are the arm bones without an exit

In the bright green tree of a child's drawing
are the old ripe apples round and red
and yellow all along on the empty branches.

Willow, New York, November 16, 2001

Song of the Beech Copse

for Naomi Burns

What blue
what russet
what whispering
what blue

What russet
vagrant windfall
migration of leaves
swirling circles

Russet ceiling
to russet floor
trembling choreography
what wind from the south

What blue
what russet
what whispering
what blue.

Tremper Mountain, New York, November 15, 2002

Song to the Moon

In the waning days of red October
you make the shadow of my house
a turreted castle
a walled medieval city
I am propelled to the eastern window
to see what you're up to

Upside down over rising mist
your smaller than usual size,
a yellow half–penny
nailed to the sky,
your intentional remoteness—you're
up to something, moon.

I'm watching.

Willow, New York, October 2002

Ode to the Old Willow

for Pablo Neruda

Protecting us from the sun
is a four-armed witness
of a former time,
two centuries back, when horse
and wagon owned these hills

Your new spring willow wands
greening
waterfall hair, your stance
a staunch defense of stable beauty,
apple-hearted

Toadstools jut from your flanks
like tables—artist palettes on which is written
the message of the wind, and you
the elephantine landscape
of bark and bole

Inn for wayfaring and homecoming birds
the tweeters and the squabblers
throng your branches
the slightest breeze takes up residence
in your attic, across your knees

Sentinel of water, your feet
are rooted in oceanic dreams
queen of gentleness, lighthouse
of security
grand aunt of the lawn, you carefully
shelter contemplative picnickers
and the good news of morning.

Kerhonkson, New York, May 2004

Scramble

You'd think
with fall protracted and the extra weeks
of Indian summer it would be finished,
but I think it works like the last cricket
singing in her shirtsleeves:
putting the garden to bed doesn't happen
until there's no sun left.

Rake up the dead leaves, canes, black debris
haul it out to the compost bin the way
Bolivian farmers taught you,
shovel horse manure on the bed,
put down the hay.
What the hell, dig the last bulbs in,
you never know,
they might come up come spring.
Feed the rhododendrons, the bleeding hearts
and acid-lovers, trim the stalks back,
pack the straw in high against the freeze.

What's that racket? Crows?
Remember them mating on the oak branch
in the summer? What a hue and cry they made
in the heat: Haw haw haw
really going at it, black wings
flapping, Haw haw
haw haw haw!

Pull the fence off the flower garden
but leave the last bits of color in,
pack the hay around them.
Wind the hose up, rattle the ice out,
coil it up on the top shelf in the shed,

and pull the flaps down over your ears
the wind's picked up
the sun's gone
you're in your shirtsleeves, nowhere near half done.

Willow, New York, October 2002

Chocha Beanie

"Ciocia": "Aunt" in Polish

Chocha Beanie, Aunt Sabina,
you had the best sense of humor
of all your sisters
giving the family horror stories
a funny twist so we could laugh
instead of filling up with shame or tears
You had us cackling over the kitchen table
cracking crab shells over newspapers, shaking
the family skeletons so their bare teeth clattered.

The wheel of paperbacks squealed inside
Rexall's on Bergenline Avenue, Union City.
I searched for something I had not read,
my own personal line of defense,
and thought how your comic touch was
a universal cure–all, knee deep as we were
in a gray world, how all comedians,
even Larry Abato in the fifth grade,
were real life heroes.

But things changed.
Uncle Boozie died, you became the lone
breadwinner, gloves up to your elbows you
commuted to the Indonesian Embassy in New York.
When they closed down, you applied for work
at a local amusement park, a huge step down,
surrounded by what your mother would call
the lower classes. Nobody spoke English.
You were overwhelmed and outnumbered.

One day you mimicked two Puerto Rican
women on the bus so it sounded
like clucking, fast and frantic,
you made fun of your old Indonesian boss, then
the Irish, the Italians; you put on a Stepnfetchit
drawl for all Black folks, or anyone darker
than us, and the laughter that used to color the air
turned to icy pings, I don't know how,
you shrank into an isolated homeland of yourself.

Attica C.F., Attica, New York, August 19, 2003

Alabama Hello

Down a long ribbon of highway
in March, in a pickup between two
Vietnam war buddies, hot sex on my mind,
I break out at dawn from the cramped
confinement into Alabama
and spring! The daffodils doubly welcome
after sleet we plowed through
late last night, the red dirt rich and warm

"I'll see you guys later!"
They pull off to deliver a seeder,
I stride into a neighborhood
of rickety houses already awake
and a crap game in early Sunday sun
on the sidewalk. No one looks up.
Nobody says hello.
Fifteen hundred miles! I'm thinking, standing
in the middle of the dusty road

A huge semi slowly bears down on me
the beefy driver leans out his window:
"You lost your way? You better git back
t'other side o' the highway. You don't
belong around here."
Fifteen hundred miles
for this crap? The girl, maybe nine,
pulls up on a battered red Schwinn,
pigtails all over her head in red ribbons,
brown skin, bright eyes

"Mornin'!" she shouts,
"Good mornin'!"

Eastern C.F., Napanoch, New York, June 2003

82

Not Yet

Can you believe that swollen joints
and inflamed knuckles and watery lungs
would make me want to kick the door
that hard, with the side of my foot

to open or close it, I forget which,
and of course only turning the knob
does that, so I'm standing at a threshold
a long way down, and I don't have wings

and of course I'm not leaving
in this body
hobbled and out of air
it would never serve me

skinny diminished calves
my failing strength before a grapefruit skin
me and Scott Nearing bring in
one piece of wood at a time

I've gotten crafty in using fulcrums
when that man in the movie tried to open
a bottle and cried, I understood
this world treats the old and infirm

like stooges in the land of plenty
blind deaf and dumb to us
in their midst, and I'm not ready
to be the old grandmother who

having lost the ability to crack nuts with her teeth
and chew whole blankets into chamois cloth
will walk into the woods and disappear
I ain't dead yet.

Willow, New York, February 2002

Mirror

The awkward move has its correlative
in the missing word, the thud of an ungainly retort

Beaten back by physical parameters,
hiding behind the damask napkin of constant pain,

distracted, one fetches a word from the infinitude
with the grace of a lame and clumsy dog.

Willow, New York, April 2003

Mean Ol' Badger Blues

Used to be a mountain climber, highest passes on the earth,
Said I used to be a climber, highest mountains on the earth,
Lucky now to get my boots on, half a mile all I'm worth.

Badger moves in fast as lightning, takes up lodgings
        in my shoes,
Said he moves in just like lightning through my gloves,
        and in my shoes,
Ugly name is Arthur Eyetis, I got the mean ol' badger blues.

Badger shot me in the elbow, in the wrists and, on a roll,
ran over all my fingers like a bus over my soul.
Seems my life's some kinda funnel, all ease movin'
        down a hole,

I got them mean ol' badger blues.

Plan ahead is not my forte, but I can't stand last-minute mess,
Don't know where that badger strike me next, or when,
        in what distress,
Feel caught up in regulation, like a rat pressed in a dress.

I got them mean ol' badger blues.

If you see me on the highway, sorta hobbling sorta stiff,
Badger kicked me in the shoulders, in the knees or in the hips,
I'd just love to punch his lights out, but I cannot make a fist.

I got them mean ol' badger blues.

Willow, New York, December 2003

Enid

for Enid Dame

You did a great service
plunging us through the brick wall
of the Patriarchs
to show the sweet funny
sensible woman's point of view
You did it without rancor or raising your voice,
a feat I have yet to master
You made it easier to accept those bastards
with their bony shoulders under blankets at 2 A.M.,
that pinched look about the nose and chin.
Even God has bunions.

You took us for a little walk around the neighborhood,
like Henry Miller, showing us
inside certain windows, embracing humanity
like the arms of Meridel LeSueur
across the prairie, across borders,
across the ravages of this cruel century's night.
There has always been a star,
a pearl of laughter, a broken dish
and us guffawing at our ultimate ridiculousness.
In a mammalian world peremptory orders—
unless it's *Don't jump! We love you!*—
are out of place.

Under the pitiless warmonger's sun
on our hills and valleys, then till now—
guns in the airports,
smirking Napoleon in the Oval Office,
bombs on our beautiful ancient cities—
we need shade trees, we need laughter

and running water to bring us from field to field.
I can hear your high voice in the corner
making sure no one has been left out
I can hear you as this paper sails across
the bedroom floor:
That's about it. Go back to sleep.

Willow, New York, January 18, 2004

Whole

I know a man who wiggles his hands
when he's happy. You can almost
imagine him as a rooster
getting ready to crow.

There's something about a sound well
clear all the way to the bottom
like a fabric they'd say was whole
without rent or seam

and the flood of sun, the color yellow
bells in the backyard
the salve of grace on the solar plexus,
Christ in the here and now.

I know a man with horns on his forehead
as plain as Moses, without regret
or apology—he's as surprised as anyone,
his face flushed with desire.

I know a man who floods the marketplace
with pronouncements, only some people
see him fold up the box he stood on,
empty it into his pocket, and walk away.

The bottoms of walls are coming away
from the tops, if you notice,
almost as if clear space is what
they hide as we huddle inside.

A young boy crows, "I did it!" to
the morning wind and sun and street corner,
the man is pedaling rapidly to China on a stationary
bicycle, the steady sound of his passage down the road.

El Paso, Texas, April 13, 2004

Food Song

for Beveraly Bellinger

Mother and her earthquake footfall
Ah Ha Ha Ha!
non–territorial
tidal pool laughter

Our dreams of bread
are solitary ruminations
songs of grain, incantatory scenes
on the plates and bowls

Prayers reduced to hieroglyphics,
archaic hymns of Zeros and Ones:
"What do you choose to fill
your mouth with?"

Ah Ha Ha Ha!
  So Ham
    O Ma
    Om

Access to nourishment freedom from pain
we stumble from the crib
sharp daggers in the fingers and toes
white heat of individuation

Unconscious to conscious song
accompanies the plough
in furrows through settled fields
in praise of the cradle of corn and beans

Ah Ha Ha Ha!
  So Ham
    O Ma
    Om

Sound itself is her form
creating sustaining
holding up the earth
pulsing in our ears

Radiant splinter
in the wing bone
speaks of a fall from grace
and subsequent return

Ah Ha Ha Ha!
  So Ham
    O Ma
     Om

Stone propped under the skull
carton of yogurt under the bed
scholars are quick to point out glyphs
in the libraries behind the gates and chains

messages spelled out in Xs and Os
devotionals to food for the mouth
food for the heart and brain:
"What do you choose to fill your mouth with?"

Have another cup, they sing
Ah Ha Ha Ha!
  So Ham
    O Ma
Dip another finger in the bowl.

Kingston, New York, September 7, 2003

The Great Vessel

The Great Vessel: I–IV

from the drawings of Sherry R. Selavy

A woman is riveted to the mirror. The no-nonsense set of her mouth and jaw and the focused clinical regard in the eyes behind her glasses suggest a surgical doctor. She steadies a knife against her chest. She has hung a transfusion syringe, already prepared and connected, over her shoulder. Her left hand empties the syringe, her right hand tilts the knife. The book on the dresser is open to a page of illustrations: the heart from every angle. A china nymph, the base of an ornate candelabra, is holding a stopwatch in her hand. Forceps and scissors stand in a jar of disinfectant. A large female doll, naked except for a pierced heart at her genitals, is covered with numbers and measured into segments like a map. A letter tells us it is Valentine's Day. The light is steady. It is time to cut in.

Her face wears the bewilderment and shock of vivisection. A book on the management of pain lies on the dresser. In the mirror she has cut open her chest and is measuring the incision with a ruler. The incision is square, she is pointing with her left hand to the heart, her heart. The tilt of her head beneath her lace shawl, affixed with a crown of roses, suggests the agonized regard of a witness or a mother over her wound. Or the indrawn sorrow of an anchorite, separated from what she seeks. Has she made the opening big enough? Antiseptic liniments and salves stand alongside pain pills and little candy hearts in a dish. *Sweet Heart. Lover. Valentine.* The china nymph holds an hourglass and has turned toward the doctor. The room is warm. The air is still.

The lace head-covering is around her shoulders. The dresser is a jumble of measuring instruments, elaborate scales, electro-cardiac machine, thermometer, hourglass, magnifying lenses, microscope, meat grinder, and surgical fork. The china nymph holds a caliper. The doctor's muscular hands hold onto her own heart, now outside her chest. Her thumbs dig into the middle as into a grapefruit, to split it open. Six candles waver in the currents of air. The woman bends over the task with care and determination. Outside herself the heart is a puzzle. The pain one expects to find registered in her face is subsumed in her inquiry. She must follow it through.

Her lace shawl, slightly opened, reveals her clavicles and breastbone, where the spread fingers of her right hand hold it in place. Her head is thrown back, her neck swan–like, her eyes are closed. Her crown of flowers is lit up like an aureole, the expression on her face indrawn, ecstatic. The china nymph turns toward us, holding a rose. The queen of hearts is melting in a magnifying glass. A heart–shaped candy box in a bowl is decorated with a white flower. Six flames are blown sideways in the wind, loose petals fly from the rose. The heart held out in the doctor's hand has become a wing, a cradle of light, a bubble traveling through space. It is midnight by the ancient clock. The vessel packed with muscle cells is empty enough now, filled with light, to move across the face of the sea and dissolve in love.

Willow, New York, March 18, 2002

The Green Piano

The Green Piano: II

for Bill Heine

When silence falls
in the dining room
it's the green piano:
someone has lifted the lid
and begun to play

dancers land
serious players lean their heads
to the left
a year compressed into a single rest stop
barely touches the pedals

a pulse like elastic bands
contracts and stretches the dancer's
calf muscles, a player
raises her hands above the keyboard
meteor showers in Gemini play all night long

no frog jumps in, no water sound
statues in the town square surge miraculously
forward, distant footsteps divide the stillness
into bites, the walker never arrives
the streaming helmets wear velocity

in the barely fluted edges
Opinions are divided
between full moon and empty moon
Which best purveys the empty space?
Which house is best for the Green Sonata?

Willow, New York, January 2002

Piazza della Bussola

Today love has settled in like a toothache
You could almost be on the other
side of a room
and my glance flies over
but cannot reach your arm

Perhaps this is unimportant
a yearning that settles
for the shine on the water
at the base of a Saracen wall
for the touch of infinity at the horizon

I am married to something defined by absence
perambulations late at night do not
bring me closer, do not pull me in
I check my position by the midnight star
mid–heavens, my star. I am here. Where are you?

Amalfi, July 20, 2000

Sehnsucht

for Jack Hirschman & Agneta Falk

The good life is not for me
walking and chatting under leafy trees
with my baby carriage
is a morning I have never known

A life of dreams
requires disappointment
holds the body tense—
expectancy belongs to another age

And perhaps none of us here
is normal. Perhaps we all wear
the stigmata of longing
for something

a place a time when the whole
body is wrenched vomiting
everything that is not it
everything that is not it.

Amalfi, July 20, 2000

The Serpent and Amalfi Rose

for Raffaella Marzano & Sergio Iagulli

In Trieste in 1975, the psychiatrist Franco Basaglia
fought to make insane asylums illegal;
Law #180 made it a crime to lock up the mad,
the somnolent and non-violent crazies
It freed them from labor camp conditions
to run loose on the streets of Trieste
Some patients died; survivors roamed
the city as free as dogs.

In Amalfi, near the Bay of Naples,
an almost transparent blue
speaks through the poets in their songs of home,
the body in the cathedral crypt
up on the hill, up fifty-four steps,
is said to be San Andrea,
disciple of Christ, a fisherman far from home.
Or perhaps it's John, the apocalypse rose.

In the cliffy land of thousand-year-old
Saracen towers, artisans carve roses
from native coral. Poets from distant lands
bring news of a war raining on their roofs, of bombs
with their own names on them written by other poets,
of confederacies destroyed. They know
the bombers' names, indict them in the cafes,
but the roofs will not be whole again.

Kali Ma is the name for words in Moroccan
At such a port there is bound to be intrigue
across the bay an entire mountain
burns in a crown of smoke

A woman remembers the beautifully painted
serpent on an Etruscan vase—power curled through history
and worshiped by ancestors was not always kind,
did not always wear a human face.

The woman weaves roses
from running water
and plump tides in the growing moon
In 1987 a huge wave hit Amalfi, as high
as the two- and three-story buildings
it's on all the postcards.
Why? she asks. The man shrugs his shoulders.
Who can explain the mysteries of the sea?

Amalfi, July 21, 2000

Pranu Mutteddu

for Chicco & Carla Pes

I.

Cork trees and cicadas
sawing in the Sardu sun
neolithic people of the standing stones
eighteen stones in a row like friends
who meet in the afternoon
and stand talking

you did not carve the trapezoidal
windows to be discovered
ages hence
you lived, as we, with the idea
that the present is immortal,
standing each stone in its bed
signaled your presence

Did you carve with the mother's vulva
central to your hill of worship?
Did you listen to the wind
and tally its news from far away?
Did you care for and provide
for the people—the old, the young?
Was there perfect equanimity?

I walk the circle
counterclockwise, widdershins
a lizard leaps into a crevice
the upright doorways are east and north
more stones line up south of the window
whatever else it was, this hill was a clock
a calendar, a lighthouse, and a place to dance

Remember the wild dances
where we turned as the earth
does, wheeling in concert
like stars
in exact directions? Our bodies
divined coordinates, took
sophisticated measurements, squared
the circle without stopping to think

A gray woman, thin, inquisitive
stands barelegged by the rock
her clothes the color of earth, of pounded
skin, of soaked bark in rudimentary weaving
Do you remember our patchwork quilt
on the hills, spinning and spinning
as we moved the designs?
In the dream of the yellow countryside
we leapt like clothespins
in a child's hands, circling in the sun.

II. Domus de Jana

This is all we know
it is not a grove
but a high bare windy hill
grass almost white
in the dancing fields

I circle the keystone
circle and fall, call out
as though speaking were a listening
If I've never been here before it looked
and felt and smelled exactly like this.

Sardinia, July 13, 1999

Colosseum

for Mássimo de Feo & Corine Young

After colonnades, frescoes, pieces of urn
a magnetism rustling in the dark
at 4 A.M., cobblestone alleys
the fountain half a city block wide
backed up against buildings
in the tiny square
like a giant child peeking out of a dollhouse

After obelisks, phalluses, columns
recounting the history of war
celebrating dominion
declaring the law!
I arrive at the Colosseum—
haunt of legendary spectacles, men against men,
men against packs of lions, packs of dogs—
lit up now for a theater piece

The horses who take part in the play
are tied outside, their heads are down
legs strangely still
Why aren't they moving?
Someone points out their feet
are shoeless, their hooves carved into
to hobble their moves,
to cause them pain when they run

Feronia, Mother of Animals!
Uni, Mother of Fields!
the clawless cats, the hoofless horses
the bull in every corrida in Spain
the condor tied to its back in Peru

cockfights, greyhound races
calves tethered all their skinny lives
to the side of a barn
processed veal for the prison guards
veal for the meaty swallowers

The old Colosseum lit up tonight
is very much alive
Restore the death penalty in Italy!
Shoot the kid off his motorbike
He's not wearing a helmet!

Rome, July 29, 2000

Temple of Vesta

Not troubled
not trampled down, O Vesta
in the shade of a colonnade providing
respite from relentless sun
I sit outside the fenced-in earth
with a bird in the tree
listening

Vesta Vesta without a face
the tree your sentinel
and servant
in a city of ghastly monuments
you preside unmoved
invisible
like water, without you

no life O sacred flame
no jar and no contents
indwelling power, song of the rose
I am back at your lintel
three thousand years have passed
your round house
quietude of late afternoon

Should I pick up a stone?
Should I leave one?
Will you not know I have passed here,
me, your daughter?
Gulls crisscross your piazza
ages of man roll out
come back like waves of the sea

You sit inside the stone well
cupped hand
ripples widening
mild protectress, mother
of the hearth, my midnight altar
an empty basket
to catch your shining grace.

Roman Forum, July 26, 2000

The Spoils of Rome

Ostentatious monuments
flung up with the wealth of
conquered nations and the strength
of slaves, one third your population,
Whatever your fame was
your moment of power,
Roman,
you are the ordinary enemy

Titans glimpsed in the street life
New York City,
gigantic forms hopping rooftop
to rooftop, and when we looked
they were fixed in place
disguised as a water tower
a top-floor landing, a wash line
and antenna.

Now against the sky huge figures
women with chariots, men with wings
the same soul-eaters of the Lower
East Side, the same cup of melancholy
competition and dominance engender
the plebian, the serf, the slave
traipsing temple to temple
ragged feet on hot paving stones

on their hands and shoulders
any praise
for the beautiful
cenotaphs

and obelisks
the giant teeth of a mighty
humorless
empire.

Rome, July 27, 2000

Eternal City

for Corine Young

On the banks of the Tevere
eternity casts its light
on the trees at 7 P.M.

traffic roaring
Caravaggio saw this light
Botticelli

last gulls patrol the surface
for dinner, hold caucuses
on the muddy bank

Roma antica
harboring a populace
over seven hills for 2500 years

blackberry canes
cut back on the bank, a flock
of tiny birds swoops and dives

gray brown with white belly bands
like little ladies in aprons
they serenade the bridge Risorgimento

little neighbors of the Tiber
hueing and crying in wide concentric
arcs from the water as high as the bridge

gold fades to rose on the ancient buildings
Michelangelo painted this light
Leonardo da Vinci

having flung themselves in controlled abandon
the birds carve out figure eights
on the water, last hosannas

Fra Angelico would have recognized,
fun in the Eternal City—
twenty of them circling in the light.

Rome, July 30, 2000

Postcard from Napoli

In the thousand–year–old seaport fortress,
in the room where Petrarch, inventor of the sonnet,
first read to the king, our performances
over, the crowds gone home,
the hours stretch out gold and blue
I would love to see you
walk through labyrinthine alleys
up to the crown of broken teeth and parapets
the whole city wears a slightly disheveled
air you with your shirt perpetually
outside your trousers would enjoy

The half moon over an alley
restaurant with two live musicians
plucking away, the holiday calm
after May Day parades,
our ferry crosses the bay
past Russian ship *Odessa*, and the blackest
of scows, *White Snow*, in the harbor,
a giant turtle in the clouds as we pulled
away, on Capri the earrings I did not buy
you would've liked these things.

Naples, May Day 2001

Verona–Heidelberg Express

for Carl Weissner

Going up over Austrian Tirol
Verona into Heidelberg
the welcome Italian sun
is having a hard time
breaking through into Germany.

The Adije river valley
full of vineyards and factories right
to the edge of the river, flowing
to the Po and then the sea, every inch
of fertile soil carefully tended
ends in snow on the slopes of Trento.

At Munich I wonder if it's latitude
jolting one into grim vistas
inside and out
Is it unremitting gray sky, November
bleakness, damp snow, fog and rain
or the certitude of every new passenger
that I've taken their seat?

Each new arrival counts the seat numbers
out loud, looks at their ticket
and then at me, *einundfunfzig,*
dreiundfunfzig, the rights
of a customer in a sensible world,
every train on time, every seat
with legitimate occupant.

In Italy, train tables were covered
with crumbs and picnic lunches
the babble of a hundred conversations
fell silent at the border

Is it latitude, nearly fifty degrees,
or barometric pressure?
Neon graffiti under bridges
was never so welcome to the passing eye.

Otto carros! Otto carros! On the autostrada
to the train I joked with musician from Trieste:
in the U.S. one car length for every ten miles
per hour is the law—eight cars at this velocity,
otto carros—a law ignored by every European driver.
How good to look for Antonio da Padova,
il santo de cosas perdutas, the saint
of lost things, including people,
and never find him.

But the university kid made sure I found
a compartment with my heavy bag,
one man helped me to heft it up,
another hoisted it down, and everywhere
I was included in the family.

Is it latitude changes this?
I am territorial as well,
protective of my private space
Is it the weather, a sky getting
dark at three in the afternoon?

Do you have a reservation for any seat at all?
the woman beside me asked pleasantly.
In fact, I do—I've been guarding it
since Brennero—
the seat across the table.
I took this one because it went forward

and when I got on another woman
had a ticket with my seat number exactly.

I figured with evident double booking
there's bound to be a randomness,
enough seats for all but perhaps not
the one you paid for,
refreshing really where everything else
is perfectly in place.

Verona to Heidelberg, December 1, 2001

Izet

In the skein of poets at a festival
under bristling eyebrows
you sing to your late wife: *200,000 women*
in Sarajevo
and none of them are you.

Bohemian in the old style
you sing seven choruses of *Bella Ciao*
at 2 A.M. on Amalfi beach, *Bella Ciao*
in a caffè in Napoli's cobblestone piazza
Bella Ciao in the pizzeria of Pistoia
Bella Ciao your eyes celebrating the new young
voices from countries whose language you
do not speak, and you are grinning
like a grandfather, *Bella Ciao*
in the banquet hall in Baronissi, Casa della Poesia,
Bella Ciao your face like Geppetto's in Swiss sunshine
with Ira Cohen, looking at the camera
with flowers in your mouth
Bella Ciao, impassioned dialogue
in the alleyways, you in Italian, me in Spanish,
Bella Ciao in sober fluorescence of tobacco shop
in Salerno, buying gifts for your grandchild,
and a nickel–plated lighter
for the army of cigarettes consumed
at the Terminus Hotel, at the train station caffè,
Bella Ciao waving at the window of the train

Bella Ciao a singing
long ago lost in my own country, Izet,
of the thousands of poets in the world
none of them and all of them
are you.

118   *Willow, New York, May 2002–March 2003*

Sarajevo Hands 2003

for Safet Zec

What can you show
but my hands covering my face?

Look at me
How will I rebuild?

In a wheelbarrow
pushing along the child

bleeding, then the old man
How will we heal?

The old shoes,
who will wear them now?

Who will wash the peppers
at the sink?

They have called up the devil
and he is speaking

English, German—what do I know?
—languages I do not understand

Hold me
while we stand like this

in the rubble where our house was,
hold me

We are made of bread,
weren't we built for freedom?

The best country in the world, if you ask,
was our Yugoslavia that was

And didn't we as a city
show the world how Jews, Arabs,

Christians, laborers and poets
could sit down together, there was

room at the table for all?
The NATO soldiers dressed as forests

have fresh round faces, they take
pictures of each other before our mosque

they carry rifles and speak in English,
German, American—what do I know?—

languages I do not understand.

Sarajevo, October 2003

Bologna Troubadour

for *Alberto Masala & Fabiola Ledd*

City of porticos
orange pink magenta
like receding vaginal tunnels
in Etruscan tombs

Head through the skylight
in ancient roof tiles, the world
above the arches clear sky
blue as Jerusalem

A warbler in the cypress
sings an irrepressible canzoneta
over neighborhood disputes in the market
gossip on street corners and

thousands of students
making their way through alleys
and corridors to the next class
in oldest university of the western world

The term "university" coined here
and the coiners buried
in prominent graves
across the churchyard

Through the skylight at midnight
motor scooters conversations cigarettes
a stillness of desert nights
above the cypress: Vega Deneb Altair

In the morning, my head thrust
into the universe again like an alchemist
into the wheeling planets,
the roof tiles moist,

the warbler
in his cypress over the convent wall
does a dozen different choruses
into the ear of the world.

Bologna, June 2004

Madre di Tavolieri

for Devorah Major & Sinan Gudzevic

I. MUSEUM

You are drawing your breath in
waiting for the sighs of the wind
to aid in childbirth
you are looking years ahead to children
who will lie down in chaos without you

You have tilted your head back
under the sky, your eyes closed
zigzags under your breasts
your hand pulling up grain
your hand pouring out oil

Tiptoeing up the steps behind museum
guard so no one will follow, we climb
back through time, up the stories
of Napoli's Archaeological Museum
we are looking for traces

You are written in the pots, the skein
of water, the zigzag of mountains
the wavy scrawl celebrating plenty
and on the top floor the photo of your
Mesolithic urn, Madre di Tavolieri.

In the urn on the side of a hill
they found you
among the things of the dead
your mouth a round O
you could almost be sleeping

dreaming in the somnolence
of another time, of intuition clouded
when we would turn away, Potnia Theron,
Mother of Animals, and lie scattered
like dormant seeds on an iron plain

II. VESUVIO

So this is your mouth of Vesuvio
open to gulps of air
sea egrets
and babble of gulls
So this is your cauldron

a vacant space
in the lava pellets
the rosy rock
of your mouth speaks volumes
like the indrawn breath of the dead

Holes in the stones
your empty eyes
closed eyelids, the skin
between us
and your interior dream

Gray wisps of smoke
from the side of your mouth
waft through the rubble
as through a veil
What do you see

in the babble of multitudes?
Children scrambling on your back
serious climbers with picks and rope ladders
thousands millions billions of us
Mater Matuta, take us back to your hands.

Naples, April 28, 2001

Across the Table

Niente e più bello che una tavola piena di
poeti pazzi.
*Nothing is more beautiful than a table full of crazy
poets.*   —*Jack Hirschman*

I'm reading your poems
and a huge ramshackle building appears, the light from a
               hundred candles
spills out on the snow. Inside at the long table Bolsheviks built
like fireplugs hammer out their arguments with Dostoevsky
               youths
and socialists from a score of countries.
The blue black skin of the Tuareg singer gleams with Saharan
constellations as he sings the language of the wind,
the one his mother taught him, the one forbidden in school.
Poets grouped together lift their glasses of grappa and
               sing along.
At the far end, intellectuals cozy up over the finer points,
               the hidden
references and underlying themes, somebody licks his fingers.
The South American woman with the voice of a train wailing
through small towns of the disappeared leans in toward
the Sikh and his syllables of Guru Nanak.
The Siberian shamaness creates in her song a mask of knotted
string through which we watch the procession of animals over
the northern vastland. A courtship dance of apples begins
               at dawn.
Three youths with a shrieking soundtrack shout simultaneous
personal histories of the horrors of war.
There's something about the cavernous heart
where all songs gather,
Bella Ciao, the *Internationale*, the jazz riff and the lullaby
the drama of hands over a table among the deaf and
               the singing.

126

The key is in the diamond in the door,
Open up it's me.
In the poem that holds the door ajar,
Ahh, we've been waiting.

Willow, New York, May Day 2003

Photo: Max Schwartz

JANINE POMMY VEGA met the writers of the Beat Generation—Herbert Huncke, Elise Cowan, Ray and Bonnie Bremser, Gregory Corso, Jack Kerouac, Allen Ginsberg, Peter Orlovsky—in New York City when she was sixteen. She lived with Allen and Peter until they left for India in 1961; by that time they had become friends for life. In 1962 she married the Peruvian painter Fernando Vega, with whom she traveled for three years through Europe and Israel. She then lived in San Francisco, where her first book, *Poems to Fernando*, was published by City Lights in 1968. From 1971 to 1975 she taught English in Peru, Colombia, and Bolivia, and for eighteen months lived as a hermit among the Aymara people on the Island of the Sun in Lake Titicaca. There she finished work on *Journal of a Hermit* (1974) and *Morning Passage* (1976).

Upon returning to America she began to work in Arts in Education programs in public schools and in writing workshops in New York State prisons. Since 1987 she has been the director of Incisions/Arts, which brings writers into prisons to perform, teach, and lead poetry workshops. She has been part of the Harvest Moon Collective, a writing group at New York's Eastern Correction Facility, since 1997. She currently teaches inside two other New York prisons for the Bard Prison Initiative.

Her travels in the 1980s and 1990s—in England and Ireland, through the Amazon jungle, in the Peruvian Andes and the Himalayas in Nepal—resulted in *Drunk on a Glacier, Talking to Flies* (1988), *Island of the Sun* (1991), *Threading the Maze* (1992), *Red Bracelets* (1993), and the prose memoir *Tracking the Serpent: Journeys to Four Continents* (1997). In 2000 Black Sparrow Press published her major collection *Mad Dogs of Trieste: New & Selected Poems*. Frequent poetry tours through Italy have occasioned two translations of her work: *To You on the Other Side of This* (2000) and *Nell'era delle cavallette* (2002).

She has received grants from the New York State Council on the Arts, the Puffin Foundation, the New York Foundation for the Arts, and the Golda Foundation. She performs her work—in English and in Spanish, with and without music—around the world.